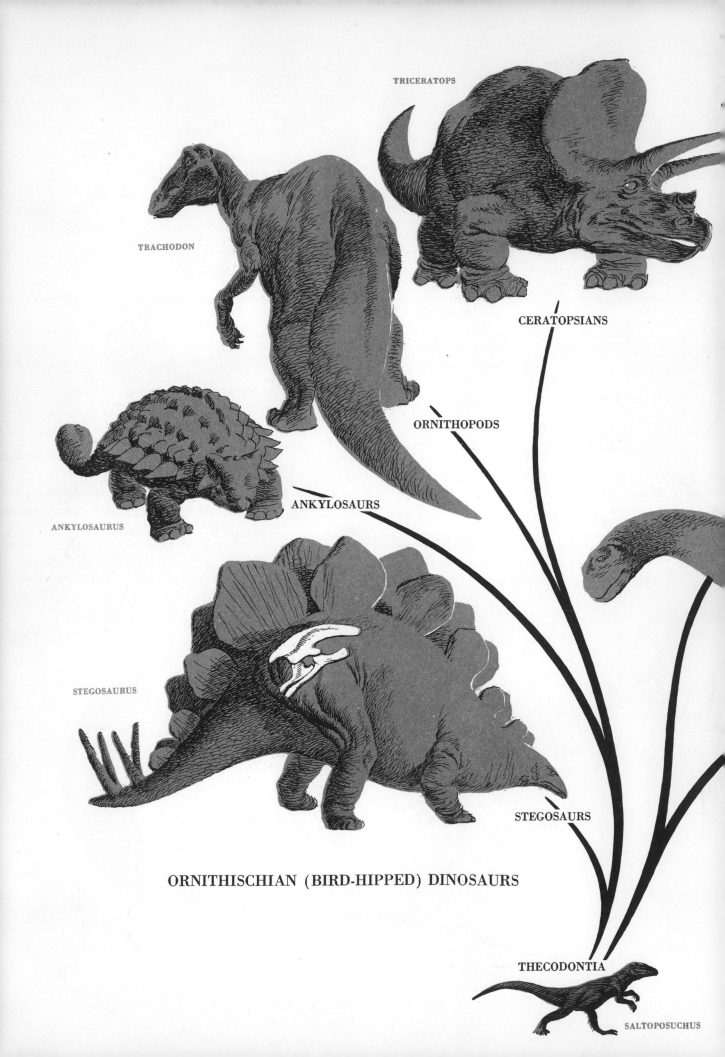

TRICERATOPS

TRACHODON

CERATOPSIANS

ORNITHOPODS

ANKYLOSAURS

ANKYLOSAURUS

STEGOSAURUS

STEGOSAURS

ORNITHISCHIAN (BIRD-HIPPED) DINOSAURS

THECODONTIA

SALTOPOSUCHUS

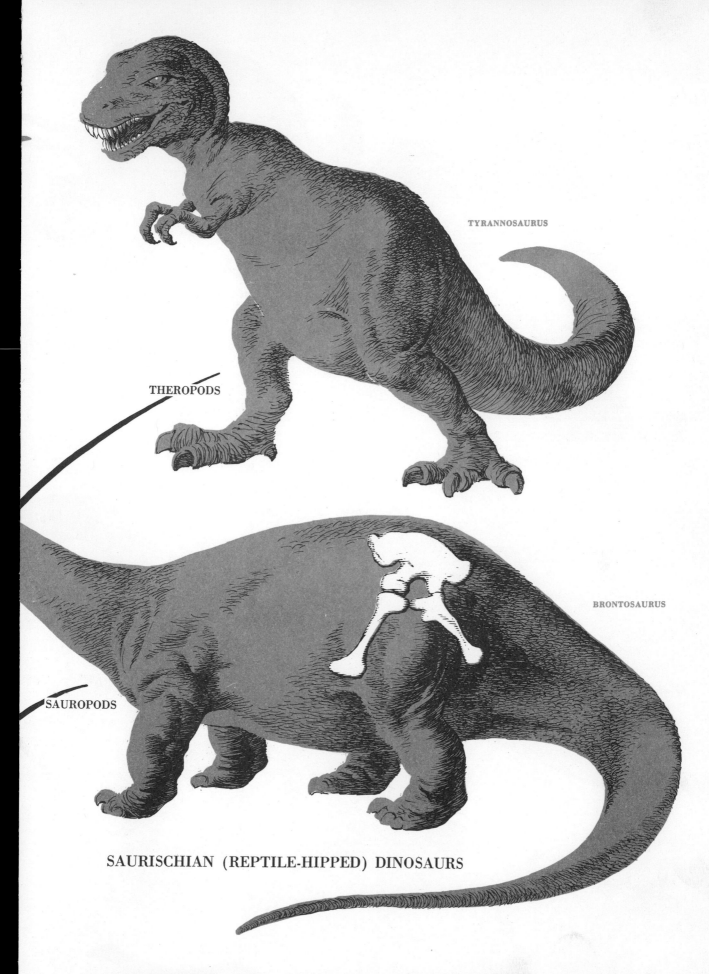

TYRANNOSAURUS

THEROPODS

BRONTOSAURUS

SAUROPODS

SAURISCHIAN (REPTILE-HIPPED) DINOSAURS

THE DINOSAUR FAMILY TREE SHOWING THE TWO ORDERS OF DINOSAURS

To Jane...a mammal

Checked for technical accuracy by Georg Zappler
Department of Vertebrate Paleontology
American Museum of Natural History

Parents' Magazine Press
52 Vanderbilt Avenue, New York 17, N.Y.

THE
RISE AND FALL
OF THE
DINOSAURS

written and illustrated by Anthony Ravielli

Buried in the crust of the earth lies one of the great unsolved mysteries of nature—the disappearance of the dinosaurs. The story you are about to read explores some of the most important theories about the destruction of these giant reptiles that once dominated the earth.

Millions
and millions of
years ago...

...long before there were any people, the world was ruled by enormous reptiles. The land they walked on trembled, and the insects and tiny mammals that shared this kingdom trembled with the land.

Among these reptiles were the biggest, mightiest, and most ferocious kings that ever lived. They reigned without rivals for millions of years. And then, suddenly, they vanished.

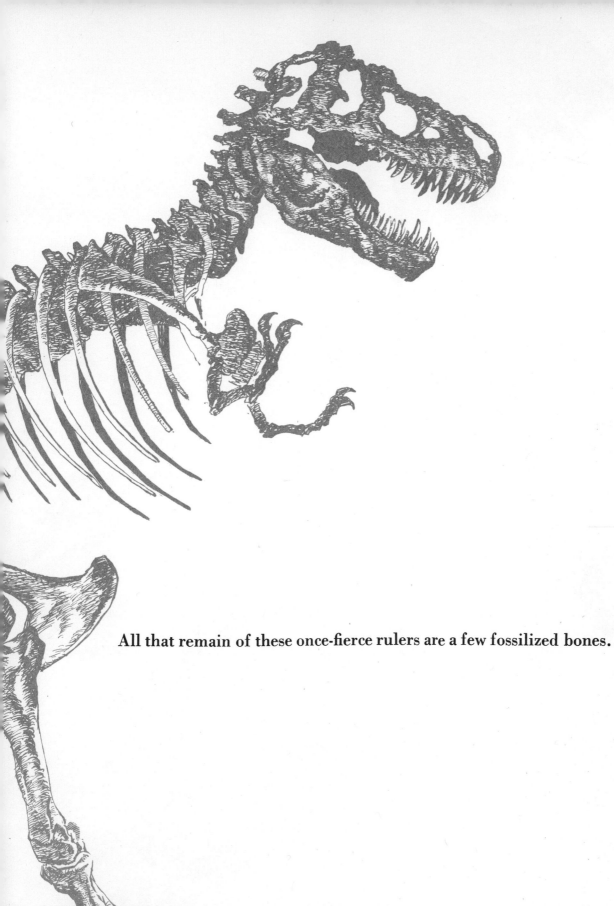

All that remain of these once-fierce rulers are a few fossilized bones.

How did this happen? We don't really know. But we do know that the giant reptiles we now call dinosaurs were wiped off the face of the earth, while creatures smaller than mice survived to inherit the world.

But let us begin at the beginning.

Geologists have divided the history of the earth into many eras, and the eras into periods. The Mesozoic era was the Age of Reptiles. It began 220 million years ago and ended 150 million years later. It consisted of three periods: the Triassic, the Jurassic, and the Cretaceous. Each of these periods lasted millions of years.

MAN   MAMMALS

GEOLOGIC TIME IS MEASURED
IN MILLIONS OF YEARS

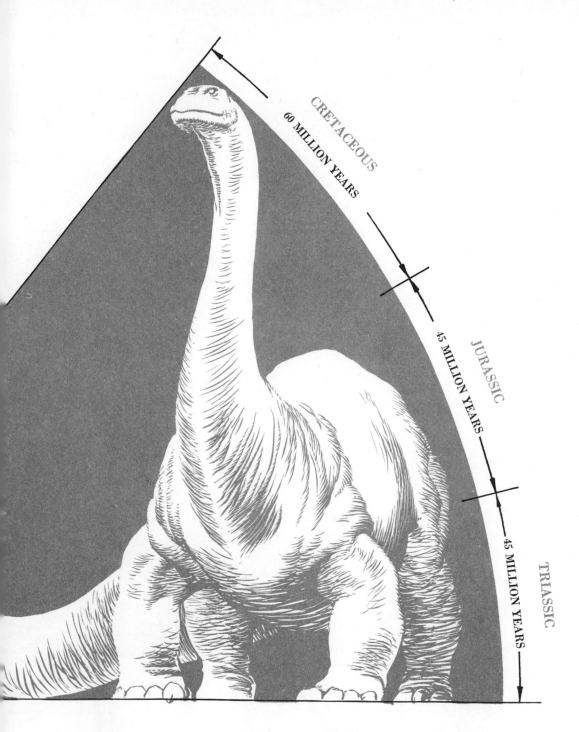

CRETACEOUS
60 MILLION YEARS

JURASSIC
45 MILLION YEARS

TRIASSIC
45 MILLION YEARS

THE AGE OF REPTILES

The world of 220 million years ago was entirely different from the world of today. There were no seasons; it was always summer. A lot of the land as we know it now was underwater. Growing everywhere were strange fernlike plants and primitive evergreen trees. Flowering plants, which are so familiar to us, did not exist.

It was in this warm, swampy world that the ancestors of the dinosaurs made their first appearance. Most of these reptiles, like Saltoposuchus, were no longer than three or four feet. Yet, they were the original models from which all future dinosaurs evolved.

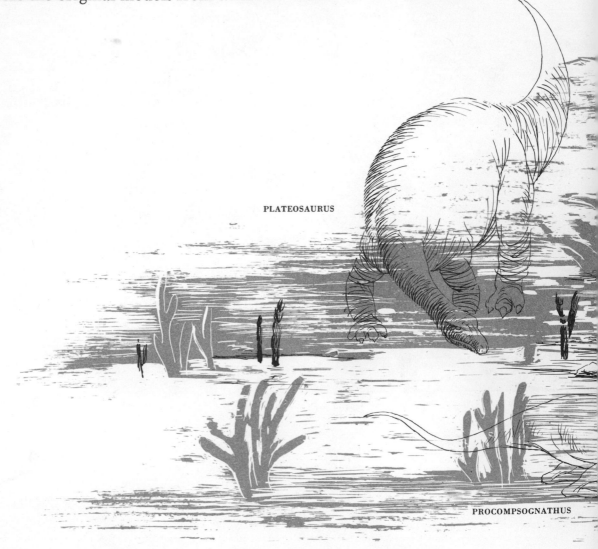

PLATEOSAURUS

PROCOMPSOGNATHUS

SALTOPOSUCHUS

By the end of the Triassic period, dinosaurs had grown in number and size. The largest creatures that ever roamed the earth were plant-eating dinosaurs called sauropods. The great Brontosaurus that lived during the Jurassic period was a member of this group. It was seventy feet long and weighed thirty-five tons, which is the total weight of seven full-grown elephants! It had a small head at the end of a long snakelike neck. Its legs, as sturdy as the trunks of oak trees, could barely support its ponderous body and tail. Brontosaurus spent most of the time in swamps and lakes feeding on soft vegetation.

CAMPTOSAURUS

TRACHODON

There were many types of plant-eaters. Some, like Campto-saurus, had powerful hind legs and stubby front limbs. It was just as easy for Camptosaurus to run or stand erect on its huge hind legs as it was for it to get down on all four feet and feed on plants that grew close to the ground. Others, like Trachodon, were duck-billed, which enabled them to feed off the bottom of swamps and shallow lakes.

As huge as most plant-eating dinosaurs were, they did have a deadly enemy—the meat-eating dinosaurs, called theropods. Here, indeed, were the rulers of all these giants that terrorized the land.

Theropods were the hunters and all the plant-eating dino-saurs, including even the largest sauropods, were the hunted.

Allosaurus, the fiercest enemy of Brontosaurus, was thirty feet long. This majestic tyrant reigned during the Jurassic period and lived on a rich diet of plant-eating dinosaurs.

ALLOSAURUS

Long after the reign of Allosaurus, the most gigantic killer that ever lived came upon the scene. This was Tyrannosaurus, the largest member of the theropod family. Its terrifying roar was first heard at the beginning of the Cretaceous period, and it thundered over the land until the last dinosaur disappeared sixty million years later.

Tyrannosaurus, known as the "king" of dinosaurs, measured fifty feet from nose to tail. It walked upright and held its terrible head twenty-five feet above the ground. The short, almost useless forelegs were in sharp contrast to the massive, muscular hind legs. Cruel, sharp claws curved out of the toes. Its murderous mouth, armed with rows of six-inch dagger-like teeth, was almost as large as its enormous head.

STEGOSAURUS

ANKYLOSAURUS

How did the plant-eaters protect themselves from the flesh-eating dinosaurs? Many, like Brontosaurus, had no other protection than the water. When a meat-eater approached, the plant-eating giants would go out into the deepest part of the lake or swamp where the carnivorous dinosaurs could not follow.

Stegosaurus, a fifteen-foot dinosaur that lived toward the end of the Jurassic period, was the first of the vegetable-eaters that had a form of protective armor. Lining the entire length of its back was a double row of upstanding flat, bony plates. On the tip of the tail were four menacing spikes that fanned upward. But this armor did not protect the tender, exposed flanks from the ripping attack of the meat-eaters.

Later, in the Cretaceous period, many new species of armored dinosaurs evolved. One of these, Ankylosaurus, had bony plates and spikes protecting its head and body. A clublike tail helped Ankylosaurus defend itself.

Another group of dinosaurs had neck shields and horns to keep their attackers away. Triceratops, the largest of this group, had a large bony hood that protected its short fat neck. Directly above the parrot-like beak was a stubby, pointed horn, and reaching three feet out of the skull, above the eyes, were two other menacing horns. The head and hood were fully one third of its twenty-foot length.

Triceratops was not a fighter. It was clumsily built. Yet, its size, weight, leathery hide, and weapons made it as dangerous to face as an armed tank. The hungry meat-eaters must have waged some mighty battles to down such creatures as Triceratops.

TRICERATOPS

The insects and the tiny mammals that shared the kingdom of the dinosaurs during the major part of the Age of Reptiles were too small to be regarded as either enemies or food by the largest dinosaurs. Nevertheless, these creatures were engaged in their own struggle for existence.

The mammals were mouselike creatures that differed from the giant reptiles not only in size and shape, but also in the way they were born.

Dinosaurs laid eggs, and from these eggs, other dinosaurs were born. These mighty reptiles had no instinct to protect their young. The world was strewn with nests containing eggs that were left to hatch by themselves.

But the little mammals did not lay eggs. Instead, their young were already formed at birth. Unlike the reptiles, the mammal mothers nursed their young and protected them until they were able to care for themselves.

The tiny mammals must have been terrified by the dinosaurs. How easily they could have been crushed to death by the enormous weight of these giants! Their lives depended on keeping out of the way of the huge but dull-witted reptiles.

Dinosaurs lumbered over the land in constant
search of special foods they needed to satisfy their
gigantic appetites.

Mammals, on the other hand, had to eat and then run back into their holes in the ground for protection. Because of their size they were always in danger. They plundered the earth for food. Having no special diet, they ate everything that could be found easily. In addition to worms and insects, the eggs of the dinosaurs fell prey to these small, nervous, always-hungry mammals.

Although we have no way of being certain, the war for the possession of the earth may well have begun during the Cretaceous period.

Yet, this was when dinosaurs, reaching the height of their glory, spread all over the world.

The hungry mammals and the indifference of the dinosaur mothers had little effect on the total dinosaur population...

...even though there may have been times when only one dinosaur was born out of all the eggs laid in dozens of nests.

Throughout the Cretaceous period, the earth itself was changing its face. Mountains rose from the flat ground. Earthquakes shook the land. Volcanoes rumbled. Swamps and shallow seas made way for plains and woodlands. Areas that were once warm and damp were now cool and dry.

The world, toward the end of the Cretaceous period, no longer resembled the early Triassic world in which dinosaurs evolved. The drab, primitive vegetation of the Triassic and Jurassic periods was replaced by colorful, flowering plants. Temperatures were no longer uniform. Upland areas were cooler than lower swamplands.

Most of the early species of vegetarians had long since disappeared. But many plant-eating dinosaurs, like Triceratops, that had evolved in early Cretaceous times adapted to these drastic changes. And as long as there were plant-eaters around, Tyrannosaurus and his meat-eating relations thrived.

But the world changed even more at the very end of the Cretaceous period. It became a world without dinosaurs.

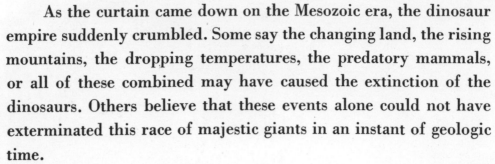

As the curtain came down on the Mesozoic era, the dinosaur empire suddenly crumbled. Some say the changing land, the rising mountains, the dropping temperatures, the predatory mammals, or all of these combined may have caused the extinction of the dinosaurs. Others believe that these events alone could not have exterminated this race of majestic giants in an instant of geologic time.

But the day did come, in that dim, distant past, when the plant-eating dinosaurs were no more. And when they went, Tyrannosaurus was doomed. It may well be that the age of dinosaurs ended with a deafening roar as the last of these tyrants killed and consumed each other.

When the last dinosaur died, 150 million years of reptile domination came to an end. In the silence that followed, the tiny, mouselike mammals that had stayed in the background throughout most of the Mesozoic era came out into the open. Before long, they overran the earth, and in time took over the world. They developed an endless variety of species, replacing the dinosaurs on every level as the dominant land animals. But would this have happened if dinosaurs had not vanished so completely?

The sudden disappearance of the dinosaurs remains one of the most baffling of nature's unsolved mysteries. We will never know if the tiny mouselike mammals hastened their departure.

But this is certain: Millions and millions of years ago, long before there were any people, there were millions of dinosaurs, and they ruled the world...

...And now there are none.

RHAMPHORHYNCHUS

PTERANODON

ICHTHYOSAURUS

GEOSAURUS

ELASMOSAURUS

TYLOSAURUS

To all grandmothers who will be completing this book,
I am five times lucky and will be filling in
five copies of this book as soon as it is published!
Lots of photographs to copy, hours
telling each newly-loved little person about my life....

And because I, and each one of us, don't have perfectly
conventional lives, I will cross out some of the headings
– and put beautiful letters from my sons and husband
over some of the pages that don't apply to my life.

I encourage you to change the book to fit your life –
some of you may have been divorced,
or may have adopted children.
Glue totally unsuitable pages together! Indeed,
glue in pages of special memorabilia and
cross out headings that don't work for you.
You can even glue a photograph of yourself over
this introduction. The *more* messed-up,
crossed out and personal your final gift is,
the more precious, the more genuine it will be.

Helen Exley

with love for

_____

from

_____

date

_____

OTHER HELEN EXLEY GIFTBOOKS:

To a very special Grandma
The love between Grandmothers and Grandchildren
To a very special Granddaughter
To a very special Grandson
My daughter, My Joy
To my daughter with love – a mother remembers
(in the same size and format as this book)

Published simultaneously in 2007 by Helen Exley Giftbooks in Great Britain,
and Helen Exley Giftbooks LLC in the USA.

ILLUSTRATED BY JULIETTE CLARKE
WRITTEN BY PAM BROWN AND HELEN EXLEY

My thanks to Pam Brown, your assistance was invaluable to me – Helen Exley
Dedicated with great love to Kezia, Jasper, Oskar, Kane and baby Rudi

2   4   6   8   10   12   11   9   7   5   3

ISBN 13: 978-1-84634-146-5

Helen Exley Giftbooks, 16 Chalk Hill, Watford, Herts WD19 4BG, UK

www.helenexleygiftbooks.com

Grandmother Remembers

Written with love for my grandchild

A HELEN EXLEY GIFTBOOK

Contents

GREAT GRANDMOTHER	GREAT GRANDFATHER
Carol	Pete

GREAT GRANDMOTHER	GREAT GRANDFATHER
Dorothy	alfred

GRANDMOTHER	GRANDFATHER
me	mike

Yₒu are woven
from a thousand lives
– the family that came before you.
Each has given you a gift –
each has played
a part in what you are.

GREAT GRANDMOTHER

GREAT GRANDFATHER

GREAT GRANDMOTHER

GREAT GRANDFATHER

GRANDMOTHER

Vickie

GRANDFATHER

MOTHER

Michelle

FATHER

Bill

NAME

Kelsey

YOUR FAMILY TREE

There has never been anyone quite like you.
You took a little from everyone who came before you.

*L*ook back, my love,

and see the procession

of your ancestors

– each handing on

their memories,

their dreams

– each now a part of you.

My grandparents

My grandparents' details

When and how they lived

My grandfather earned his living

Their talents

My grandparents' details

When and how they lived

My grandfather earned his living

Their talents

Health history and important information

Things I've been told about them

When my grandparents lived

What I remember of them

Things I've been told about their lives and families

Living conditions for our family

How things were different for them

New inventions and changes in their lifetime

Great social changes and events in their time

Important events in their lives

How they spent their lives

What opportunities existed for women?

Great achievements

Great losses

Important events

Other information about my grandparents

PHOTOGRAPHS OF MY GRANDPARENTS

OLD FAMILY PHOTOGRAPHS

History of my family

Earliest known history and origins of the family

Great historical events – wars, peace, natural disasters that affected our family

Social changes that affected us

Financial background and changes in our family

Important family events

Medical histories, causes of death

Occupations

Talents and achievements

Other stories and memories

The world when my mother was young

The great world events when she was a child

How world events affected my mother and her family

Great world events when she grew up

The medical advances and how they affected her life and world

The great inventions in her life

When radio, electricity, cars came...

Books/great people who changed her life

The political changes in her lifetime

My mother

Her maiden name

Why her first names were chosen

Her birth date, birthplace and important facts

Her education

Family life

Her greatest adventures

Her talents and skills

Stories she told

Her hopes, dreams and plans

The things she liked and disliked most

The things she feared most

Her hardest times

Her funniest memories

Her happiest times

Her greatest achievement/s

Other important facts and events

My father

Why his first names were chosen

His birth date, his birthplace and important facts

His education

His greatest achievements

His greatest disappointments

His talents and skills

His hopes, dreams, plans

Things he liked and disliked most

Things he feared

His hardest times

His happiest times

His funniest stories/memories

Other important and interesting things

PHOTOGRAPHS OF MY MOTHER

Becoming a woman

My mother's best stories about growing up – as a woman

The barriers most women faced

The obstacles she faced

The dreams...

What she has overcome as a woman

What she taught me about my role

How things have changed for women as I grew up

What obstacles remained for me

My successes and failures

My parents' wedding

My parents' wedding day

How my parents met

Stories they have told of their romance and courtship

What my mother told me about her wedding day

Marriage and home

Where my parents lived

What their home/s looked like

Their financial state

Their struggles

Their successes

What occupation/s they had

What they liked about each other

How world events affected their lives

What I have heard of their life together

Stories about the family – and special memories

PHOTOGRAPH OF ME AS A CHILD

Me!

The names I was given when I was born

The reason for those names

My pet names, my nicknames

Important facts

Memories of when I was very young

What I disliked and feared

Stories about me as a baby

Stories about me as a child

The best of my memories

Memories of my childhood

Our family

Brothers, sisters, and relations

Early adventures

Sad times

Happy times

Things that formed my character

My first loves – flowers, books, animals...

My early talents

Things I most disliked

Things that hadn't been invented then

Things about me then that changed a lot

Things I'll never forget

PHOTOGRAPHS OF ME AS A CHILD

My school days

My best subjects

School work I most disliked

My talents and achievements

How I got to school

What school was like when I was young

What is better at schools today

What is worse in schools today

What were school rules that aren't here today

What was discipline like then

What made me laugh

Memories you would like to hear

PHOTOGRAPH OF ME AT SCHOOL

When I was young

The first sight of the sea

Learning to swim/play sport

My first dance

Music, books that I loved

Travel memories

First successes

My early failures

My best memories

My early strong values and beliefs

A PHOTOGRAPH OF ME AS A TEENAGER AND YOUNG WOMAN

My first passions and major interests

Other special firsts

My dreams

What I dreamed about

People, books, events, music that made me dream

What I wanted to be

My hopes for the world and what I believed in

My concerns – political, social, personal

Anxiety and excitements about growing up

Broken dreams

Dreams that have stayed with me

Love and romance

How I met your grandad

What I remember about falling in love

What I most liked about him

What he most liked about me

Romantic moments

Our song, our special places

The things we did together

Some obstacles and problems we overcame

Unforgettable memories

Our hopes and dreams

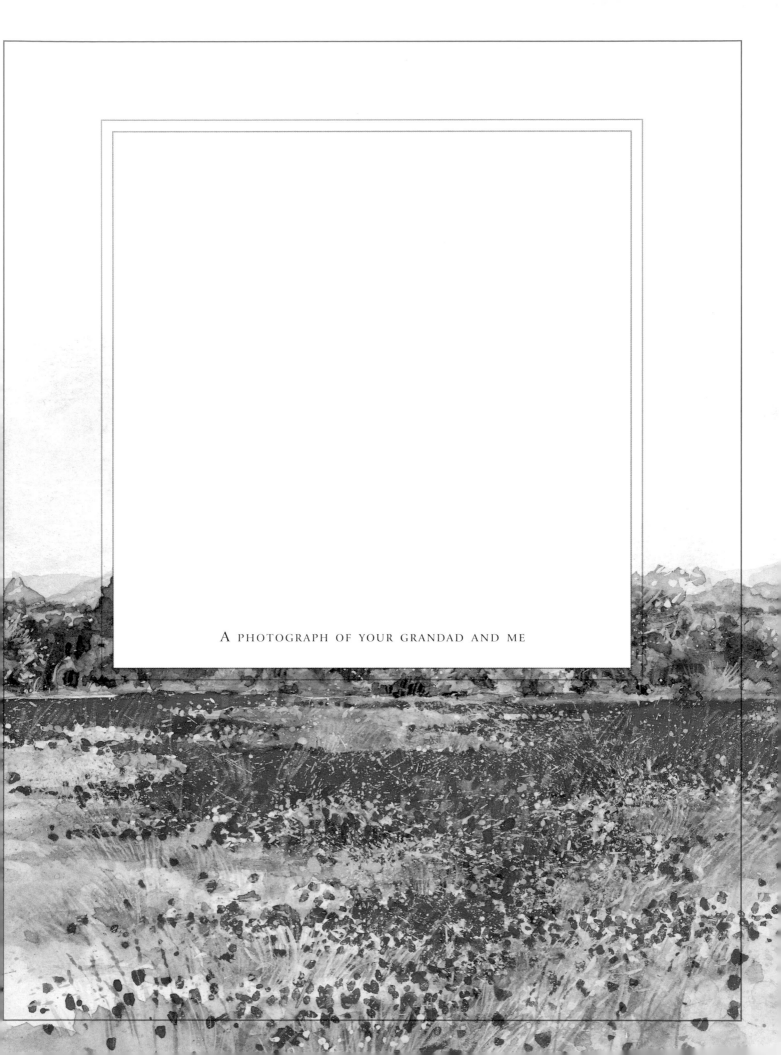

A photograph of your grandad and me

My wedding

The date and place of our wedding

Your grandfather's full name

About him – his life, his work, his family

What the wedding was like – my dress, the reception, the music and all the details

Description of my special, my lovely, day

Things that went wrong!

My happiest memories

PHOTOGRAPHS OF OUR WEDDING

$\mathcal{A}$nything, everything, little or big, becomes
an adventure when the right person shares it.

KATHLEEN NORRIS (1880-1966)

PHOTOGRAPH/S OF OUR EARLY LIFE TOGETHER

Early times together

What we grew to love about each other

Where we lived, what our first homes were like

Practical early problems

How we overcame problems

Building a family

Things we bought that I still treasure

Sad memories

Wonderful memories

Your parent is born!

Your parent's birth details

Why we chose his/her first names

What/who he/she looked like

The first thoughts I had

Worrying things

Happy times

Practical problems of babies in those days

What I loved about him/her

My strongest memories

PHOTOGRAPHS OF MY CHILD – YOUR MOTHER OR FATHER

Your parent growing up

Going to school

The funniest things!

Naughty days!

Talents

Hobbies and interests

Early dreams

Greatest achievements

...and interests

What has made me most proud

A PHOTOGRAPH OF ME AND YOUR PARENT

Me and your parent

The connection I have felt

How he/she changed my life

What I've learned from him/her

What we have in common

Ways in which we are utterly different

What has made me laugh/happy

Our strengths together

Sorrows we've shared

Things we both enjoyed doing together

You!

My memories of the first time I saw you

My hopes and fears for you when you were born

How your birth changed my life

The world you were born into... world events and changes

Things that are very different to my childhood

PHOTOGRAPHS OF ME AND YOU

PHOTOGRAPHS OF YOU

You – the early years

What I thought of you

Things that made me laugh

What made me proud

Funny things you did or said

Things you loved

What we loved

What frightened you and calmed you

My happiest memories

PHOTOGRAPHS OF GIRLS AT MY TIME – OR ME

How the world has changed in my lifetime

Inventions

Household chores when I was young

Population growth and how it has changed our town, nature, shopping...

Medical cures

Transport changes

What we did for fun

The coming of television and changes to radio

Major world events that have affected my life, my family

Changes in society's values

Other important changes

Sad things

The great personal sorrows of my life

About beloved people I remember

Major events: wars, epidemics, natural disasters

Things that worry me and my fears for your world

My feelings of sadness and disappointment about the world

My beliefs, my passions

Important beliefs that have inspired my life

The great teachers

The great political leaders

Other "ordinary", very extraordinary, people in my life

Books that have changed my life

Great movies

Great artists...

Historical changes and events that have affected/changed me

Central events in my own life that have changed me

Things I have loved

Things I have loved

Movies/Shows

Music, songs

Pets and animals

Food

Flowers, trees, nature

Places, countries

Hobbies and activities

Things I'd like to share with you

The most-loved, glorious memories of my life…

I have such hopes for you – not fame or riches, though they may come, but the enthusiasm to make bold choices, to learn and experiment and make and do. To weather storms. To learn from failure. To discover goodness in other people.

A PHOTOGRAPH OF YOU AND ME TOGETHER

My hopes for you

I wish you the joy of this music I have loved

I wish you these extraordinary sights

...these books, these movies

...these special places

...moments of this kind of special love

Adventures I wish you

Things I wish I'd learned

Things I've never done, risks I've never taken that I hope you'll have the courage to

Other loves I wish you

Letters, copies of documents, photographs – extra space for everything else that's important

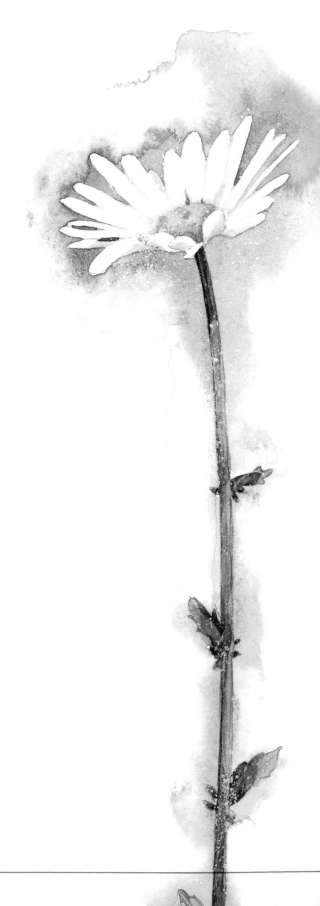

Other important extras

For your choice of press cuttings, personal thoughts,
a loved poem, a special picture....

*T*ake with you into your future all my love.
All the things we've seen together,
all the music we've heard,
all the people we have met and loved,
all the secrets, all the gigglings,
all the mischiefs we have made.
I'll come with you as far as I'm allowed
along your road –
and when we part you'll take with you
my hopes and half my heart.

Words by Pam Brown, B.1928

A letter from me to you